Arctic Hero

The Story of Matthew Henson

Alison Hawes

Contents

Great Clarendon Street, Oxford OX2 6DP

Oxford University Press is a department of the University of Oxford. It furthers the University's objective of excellence in research, scholarship, and education by publishing worldwide in

Oxford New York

Auckland Bangkok Buenos Aires Cape Town Chennai Dar es Salaam Delhi Hong Kong Istanbul Karachi Kolkata Kuala Lumpur Madrid Melbourne Mexico City Mumbai Nairobi São Paulo Shanghai Taipei Tokyo Toronto

First published 2003

British Library Cataloguing in Publication Data

Data available

ISBN 0 19 919539 0

10 9 8 7 6 5 4 3 2 1

True Stories Pack 2 (one of each title) ISBN 0 19 919544 7
True Stories Pack 2 Class Pack (six of each title) ISBN 0 19 919545 5

Acknowledgements

The publisher would like to thank the following for permission to reproduce photographs:

American Museum of Natural History: p 10; Corbis: p 19; Corbis/Bettmann: pp 25, 28; Corbis/Hulton Deutsch Collection: p 7; Corbis/Staffan Widstrand: p 9; Mary Evans Picture Library: pp 1, 29; National Archives Peary Collection: p 23; Science Photo Library: p 13; Stone: p 3; TNT Originals Inc: p 30.

Front cover background artwork : Corel Professional Photos
Inset photo: Corbis/Bettmann
Back cover: Mary Evans Picture Library.

Illustrations are by Ann Baum

Printed in Great Britain by Ashford Colour Press, Gosport, Hants

Introduction

In 1909 a black American explorer called Matthew Henson helped to discover the **North Pole**.

This story tells you how Matthew became an explorer and the dangers he faced in the bitter cold of the **Arctic**.

Matthew spent many years exploring the Arctic.

Chapter 1

Running Away

As a boy, Matthew always longed for adventure.

When he was about 12 years old, he ran away to sea. He joined a ship as a cabin boy, peeling potatoes and cleaning the decks.

When he left, at the age of 18, he had already travelled the world.

Chapter 2

Matthew Meets Robert Peary

A few years later Matthew was working in a shop when he met an explorer called Robert Peary. Robert offered him a job, as his servant, working in the jungles of Central America. Matthew was keen to travel again, so he took the job.

While they were in the jungle, one of Robert's survey team fell into some quicksand. The man was so frightened, he left the **expedition**.

Matthew asked if he could take over the man's job, and he never worked as a servant again.

After working in the sticky heat of the jungle, Robert's next trip was to the bitter cold of the Arctic. He asked Matthew to come with him as a member of his team.

He and Matthew then spent the next 18 years exploring the Arctic together.

Robert Peary

Chapter 3

Matthew in Greenland

They began by making several trips to Greenland, where the **Inuit** people helped them to learn the skills they needed to survive in the Arctic.

Matthew quickly learned to speak Inuit and became good friends with the people. They called him "Matthew-the-kind-one".

They learned how to fish for **charr** and hunt for seals.

They learned to build igloos and make clothes and boots from animal skins.

An Inuit man fishing for charr.

They also learned to build sledges and drive teams of **husky** dogs. In fact, Matthew soon became an expert sledge driver.

Matthew and Robert travelled across the unexplored ice fields in the north of Greenland. They made maps and helped to show that Greenland is an island. They also found three enormous **meteorites**.

A meteorite found by Matthew and Robert is now in the American Museum of Natural History.

But even with help from the Inuit, the Arctic was a dangerous place for Robert and Matthew to be.

Once they were out hunting when a musk ox suddenly charged at Robert. Just in time, Matthew saved Robert's life. He shot the ox with his last bullet.

Another time they were hundreds of miles from camp when they ran out of food. They were cold and weak, and a man travelling with them was dangerously ill. In the end they had to eat their dogs or starve to death.

Chapter 4

To the North Pole

Despite the dangers, Robert and Matthew bravely went back to the Arctic again. This time they wanted to do something no one had ever done before. They wanted to try to reach the North Pole. But on their first attempt Robert's feet became badly **frostbitten**.

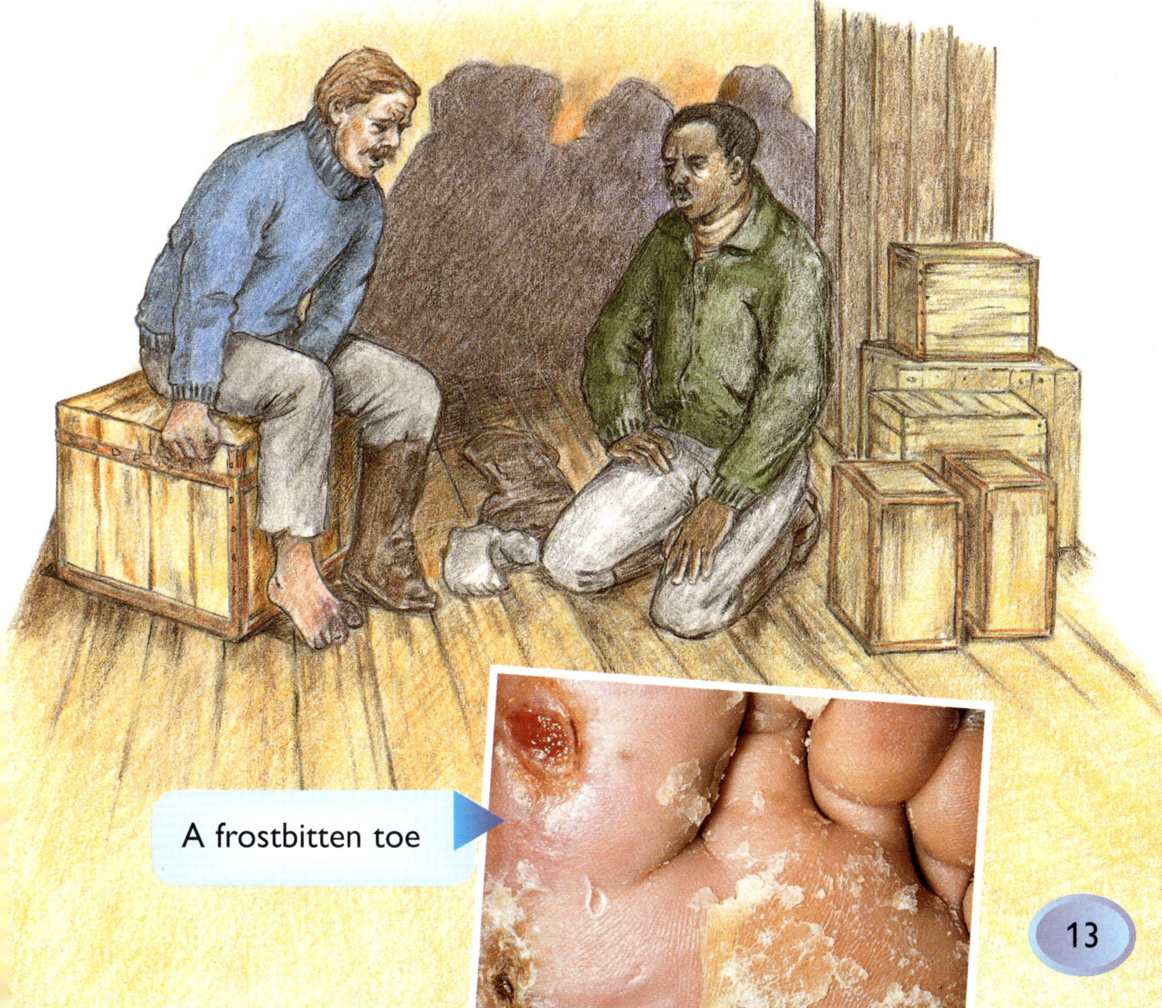

A frostbitten toe

Robert was in such pain that he couldn't walk or even stand.

As soon as they could travel, Matthew strapped Robert to a sledge and rushed 250 miles to base camp, where there was a doctor. The doctor had to take off eight of Robert's toes.

But still Robert and Matthew would not give up. Three more times they tried to reach the Pole.

Each time they got closer than before. But each time they were beaten back by **blizzards** or melting ice.

Chapter 5

One Last Chance

In 1908 Robert and Matthew sailed from New York to make their fifth attempt to reach the Pole. But they agreed, because of their age, that they would make this their last trip to the Arctic. This would be their last chance to reach the North Pole!

On their way north, they stopped in Greenland to buy the huskies, furs and equipment that they needed.

They also visited several villages to hire Inuit men and women to come with them and help them on their last journey.

As their ship sailed further north, the sea began to freeze over.

At first the ship was able to cut through the ice, but as the ice got thicker they sometimes had to use dynamite to help them break through.

Robert and Matthew's ship stuck in the ice

In the end the sea ice was just too thick and they could go no further. So they set up their base camp on an island off the coast of Canada.

They spent the winter getting ready for their last attempt to reach the Pole.

In the spring they were ready to set out.

Robert put the men into teams and they began setting up a line of camps across the sea ice. At each camp they left food, equipment and **igloos** for Robert and Matthew to use on their way back from the Pole.

But this was not easy. Time and time again they were held up by the ice and the bad weather. At times the ice was so jagged it broke their sledges.

Other times it was so high that they had to drag their heavy sledges over it by hand.

The ice creaked and moaned and cracked open without warning.

Once Robert was going to sleep when he heard a noise. Looking outside, he saw a crack open up around one of the other igloos! He and Matthew shouted to the men who just had time to leap to safety.

When they were 130 miles from the Pole, they set up their last camp. Robert sent the last support team back to base camp, as they were no longer needed.

Then, with Matthew and four Inuit men, he set off on the last leg of their journey to the Pole itself.

The names of the four Inuit men were (from left to right) Egingwah, Ootah, Ooqueah and Seeglo.

For once the ice was smooth and the weather good, and for the next few days the six men made good speed.

But, just a few miles from the Pole, Matthew suddenly fell through the ice. Luckily one of the men was close by and pulled him out before he drowned.

Later that day the six men reached the Pole.

It was 6th April 1909.

After years of hard work, disappointments and danger Robert and Matthew had done it at last. They were the first people ever to stand at the North Pole!

This is the actual photo Robert took of his team at the North Pole.

Chapter 6

Back Home

Matthew and Robert arrived back in New York months later, expecting to be treated as heroes. But this was not to be.

While they were away, a man called Frederick Cook had claimed to have reached the North Pole before them!

In the end, Cook's claim was shown to be a **hoax**.

Robert, being the leader of the expedition, was rewarded with the fame and medals he deserved.

But sadly in America at that time, black people were given little respect. So, at first, Matthew was not rewarded for his part in the expedition.

Chapter 7

Rewarded at Last

It wasn't until he was an old man that Matthew was given any rewards for his part in reaching the North Pole.

And even now, years after his death, the world is still only just learning about this great explorer.

Matthew finally receives a medal at the age of 81.

1866 Matthew is born

1887 Matthew goes to Central America

1909 Matthew reaches the North Pole

1860 1870 1880 1890 1900 1910 1920

Matthew runs away to sea 1878

1891 Matthew goes to Greenland

In 2000 the greatest medal an explorer could ever wish for – the Hubbard medal – was awarded to Matthew's niece on Matthew's behalf.

Matthew Henson – the man who helped to discover the North Pole – would now be remembered by people all over the world!

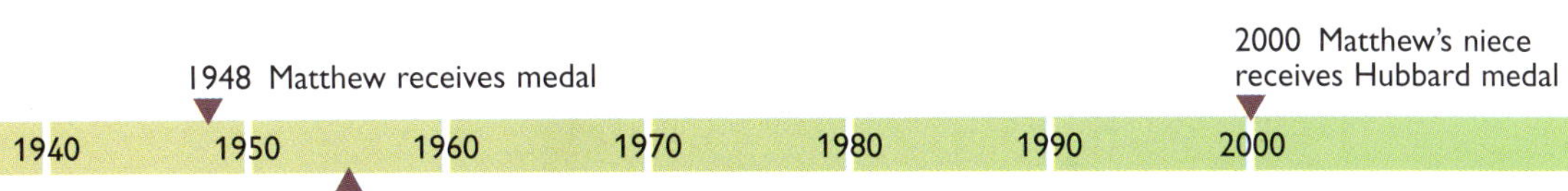

More information about Matthew Henson

In 1998 a film called *Glory and Honor* was made, claiming to be the true story of the search for the North Pole.

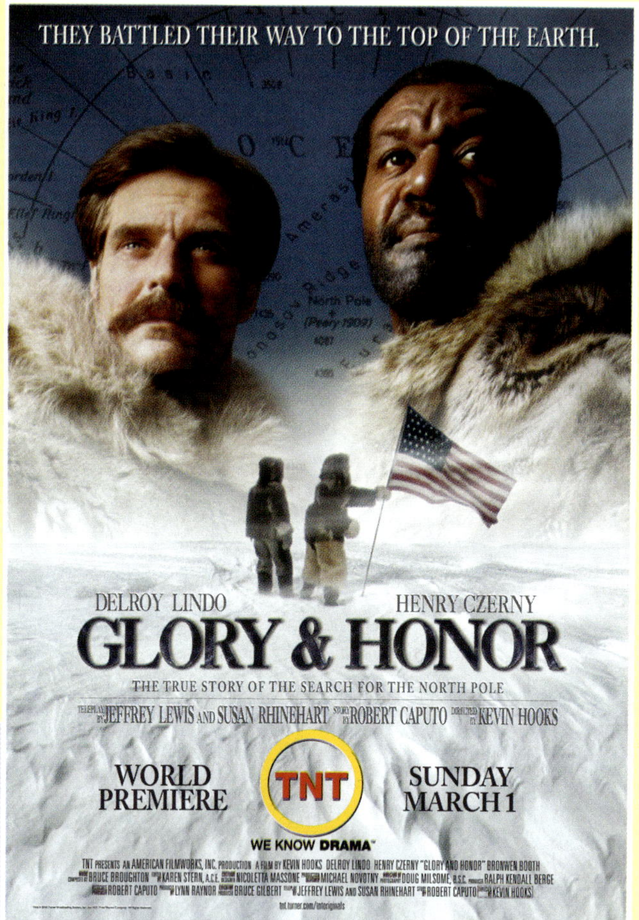

Then, in 2001, a radio programme called *Stealing the Glory* was produced.

You can find more information about Matthew Henson on these websites:

www.matthewhenson.com
www.unmuseum.org/henson.htm
www.matthewhenson.org

Glossary

Arctic the name given to the land and sea around the North Pole

blizzard a very bad snowstorm

charr a fish found in the Arctic

expedition a long journey made for a special reason

frostbite an injury to part of the body when it becomes frozen

hoax a lie or trick

husky the breed of dog the Inuit use for pulling sledges

igloo a shelter made from blocks of snow

Inuit the name for the native people of Greenland and Canada

meteorite a rock that has fallen to earth from outer space

North Pole the most northerly place in the world

Index